40 Jewels

Part 1

Dedications:

First, I like to thank the most high for allowing me to keep ticking. I am filled with gratitude for being able to see what I've seen and love how I've lived despite all my shortcomings. I am proud of my surroundings and the loved ones I call friends and family. Without you, there is no me. My mother, Barbara Spencer is the greatest example of strength that I have ever witnessed, and I am so thankful for her giving me life and being apart of my life to this present day. She is the chief editor of this book, as well as a huge part of my support system. We talk daily. I thank my sisters, Jennifer and Tina for being strong women in this world and taking care of their responsibilities raising my nieces and nephew. A huge part of me yearns for their acceptance and approval as they are older and wiser than me. I hope to continue to watch them navigate through this world with an abundance of love. My son John Jr. is my rock. He has kept me moving with purpose and intent for two full decades. I try to tell him as much as I can that I am proud of him. He stands on his two feet and thinks with his magnificent brain. I couldn't ask for a better man to carry on my legacy. I love, trust, and believe in him because I see the God in his stature. He has given me great purpose in this world, and I am forever grateful. My daughter JaNya is my world. I never knew I could love so deeply. A huge part of my soul would be perfectly content in just watching her be happy. I am deeply obsessed with her smile and natural grace. She doesn't know it, but she has the power to control everything in her world. She has it in her and as long as I live, I will constantly stick a mirror in her face so she can see who she is, a Godly being.

In the middle of me completing this book, I watched my father live his last days on earth in great pain. I was devastated watching him wither away. I realized during the duration of his slow death, that I loved him and valued his words. I honestly feel like he was put into my life to guide me, which he did in so many ways. I wanted him to read this book in its entirety. I wanted him to be proud, but I didn't get the opportunity to share this with him. In this book, you may feel the ups and downs I felt during this process. Some of the words you will read in this book were written as I sat by his side as he laid on his death bed. What a tough time this has been. But I must believe he is in a better place, I dedicate this book to him, Allen Spencer who is my father. He came into my world when I was five years old, and he never left until his heart stopped.

This book is in two sections, part one and part two. I felt it was important to break this up because I felt different energy. Let's dive right into part one.

Table of Contents

Introduction

As I sit here on this plane headed to Miami, I am thinking to myself this world will never be the same. COVID 19 has taken the world to another level that was unforeseen. It still seems like yesterday; we were living carefree for the most part. We would go to work, come home to our families if we had one, and live life striving to have things. We all were striving to live in a structured chaos, but nothing quite like what we are seeing today in 2020. As you turn these pages and read, please keep an open mind. I have been diagnosed with PTSD, and ADHD in previous years. I've also have had bad episodes with depression and alcoholism in the past. I used to smoke weed at an early age of 8 with my step pops. I was kicked out of every school I've went to several times (besides college) and finally expelled my junior year. The principal told the school board I needed strict, structured supervision and to never come back to Des Moines Public Schools. I've been robbed at gun point a couple of times, once with three guns to my head. I've been in near death experiences more than I could count. I have a lot to say. I want to tell the world some things that helped me get through a lot of bad situations. I can honestly say standing here today that I've never taken a loss for long. I've learned from my experiences and to me, that is the key to life. Being able to reflect, revise, revisit, and retry often is a blessing and the ingredients of living. Life. I cherish the moments I have, and I am excited you've picked this book up to give it your attention.

I write this book for you. I write this book because our time is limited on earth, and I have a burning desire to help my surroundings the best way I know how. The way I know how is by sharing my experiences and hopefully I can influence a few people to take a different route, think from different lenses, or just simply smile. This book will be timeless and can be a point of reference for so many obstacles. You will be able to take several points from this book and use them, regardless of who you are. As I've stated in other books, I am in no way claiming I know it all. I'm not the smartest tool in the shed, and I always make it my intention to never be the smartest in the room. I feel I've made more mistakes than the average, so a part of my burning desire in life is to help where I can by trying to prevent my people from making the wrong decisions. I tell my relatable past and my perspectives, which I think can be different, and less popular. Going forward, my way of thinking will provoke your thoughts. I cannot dare go through life without giving my views, and in constant search of that one person I can uplift. Maybe you are a 19-year-old drug dealer that feels like going to prison at some point is inevitable, and you don't care because you are caught up on this moment and have no feelings for the future. I want that young man to understand that was me, and I grew from that mindset to do beautiful things after I worked on my self-awareness. Maybe you are that aspiring playwright that just hasn't taken that step to produce a play. You have all the tools, and you know you write great work, but something keeps holding you from moving forward. Maybe I can spark a match that will set you on a journey to jam pack an auditorium like I once did. I produced an original urban stage play in Des Moines, Iowa, when original stage plays were not a commonality in that region. Maybe you are at age 70, and everywhere you turn, people are younger than you with a different mindset and language. You have so many gifts to give the world, but you feel like you are too old to grow. I want to convince you that you need to get out of your own way. I want to show you how your conditioned mind stops your growth. I want to help people see different views and understand our surroundings from a wider lens. Before I go, I would like to give my 2 cents of my world to all of you. I present 40 jewels in 40 years. These are lessons I've either learned the hard way, or they came with ease. These are in no order, as I believe each one is vital in this thing called life. My trials and tribulations have been big, but my outlook sees the world as manageable with these jewels. You may disagree with some of my views, and that is perfectly ok. Who agrees with someone about EVERY topic? However, having an understanding is beautiful. If you understand, you can disagree with respect. Here are the first 20, as I split this book into two parts. The reason is because I want to give you, the reader a break in between. Here I present to you, 40 Jewels! Thank you for your valuable time!

Jewel 1:

Don't Get Caught Being a Pawn on Someone's Chess Board

So, I was 19 years old working at this call center. I had a little illegal hustle going on , on the side, so I didn't look like a young man that was needing this $10.00 an hour job. I always dressed well, smelled good, and my hair was always whipped up in long braids looking "fly". I looked like a baby, even though I was a father. I had a freckled baby face, so I often would get the "oh you are adorable", instead of "you are so sexy". With my baby face, it surprised me that I was getting attention from grown women. I looked like a baller (a money getter having life his way) though. I had a couple nice cars and some nice jewelry, so getting a lady my age was not a problem. I worked at a call center full of women, and at times

I was shy. One day, I walk in and there is this lady staring at me. This lady (we will call her Bobbie) had to be about 35 years old, and she had a lovely shape. She approached me and started telling me about herself. She wasn't the most attractive woman in the world, but I was so happy I was being approached by an older woman. She had a way about her that made me feel good. She was a good seven, but her body was a 10. So, the next few days we talked at work and I can tell she was really feeling me.

One day she was so adamant about me coming over to her house that night, I was feeling pressured. I didn't know if I could make it because of my daddy obligations, but I was about to try and figure this one out. Not only was this woman older and seems like she got it going on, but she wanted to give me some play badly. I was with it. She left me a note saying, "here's my number. Make sure you come by tonight. I'm going to show you some things. It's supposed to rain tonight too." When she left me the note, she winked and walked away. I'm going to tell you the honest to God truth. I couldn't concentrate for the rest of the day. All I kept thinking about was how I was going to put the stroke game down on this potential sugar mama. I then started thinking about getting into her purse. Back then, I was always scheming on a come up and since she was older and seemed like she had it all together, I felt like she was able to invest into my hustle. I kept thinking about the game I was going to play to persuade her to come up off some money. I was totally motivated to arrange my schedule to make this move happen, so obviously you already know I made it to her house. Make a long story short, I called Bobbie once I pulled up to make sure I was good. She answered and told me to come upstairs. She lived in a decent apartment building. I got out the car, made sure I had my travel pack of condoms in my pocket, and I made it up the stairs. She let me in and I'm playing it cool for the moment. She said she cooked for me, and once I sat down, she brought me a plate. Well, usually I would be very appreciative, but in this case, I was offended. First off, my young mind was thinking, "I'm about a dollar, I don't care about your food." I couldn't wait to tell her "No, thank you. I'm good," because back then I thought it was cool to shoot down everything but a buck or some ass from a woman. On top of that, she had a fried pork chop and some broccoli and cheese. It looked so good, I couldn't even lie, however I didn't eat pork. I thought it was rude of her to just cook something for me without asking if I ate what she was cooking. But I soon figured out that she wasn't cooking for me. She didn't really care about me anyway. Ten minutes into me being there, her phone rings. She quickly picks up the phone. I hear this man yelling at her and she says, "Not right now Joe, I have company." I'm looking at her and she turns to me and tells me that it's her ex. I later find out that Joe was her husband. They were separated, but he recently moved out of the apartment. You mean to tell me I'm sitting on this man's couch? Oh, I'm about to leave. She fusses back and forth with him on the phone for the next two minutes or so. During this time, I'm thinking maybe I should just leave. I remember me standing up while she was sitting next to me. While she was on the phone, she stands up with me and starts to rub on my chest. She motioned me to sit back down. She eventually hangs up with him and we were back to talking on the couch. She tells me to not worry about him and then suddenly, there is a knock at the door. This knock sounded like the police banging at the door. "Bobbie, open up this door! I'll kick it open if you keep playing!" echoed a very deep, loud voice. Now I feel like this woman set me up. She looks at me and says, "I must let him in, but he won't get you. Don't worry, I'll handle him."

So here I am, young and looking dumb founded, sitting down with this plate of food next to me. She opens the door, and I swear it looked like the Black Hercules came through the door. This dude had to be 6'5 and had at least 2,000 muscles bulging from his upper body. I didn't have my pistol on me. This was a time period of my life where I didn't carry one every single day. But that soon changed (I explain in later chapters). Mind you, I'm about 165 soaking wet. I'm trying to be calm, and this big gorilla monster of a man comes in and grabs her and tells her to sit down. She says, "Joe, this is my good friend John. He's going to be around for a while."

"What in the hell?" I'm thinking in my head. "Good friend?? I barely know you." Joe turns to me, looks at the plate I have on the side of me, looks at me and starts balling! He turns to Bobbie and says, "Baby I love you." She says to him, "oh don't start that now, you weren't saying that when you were rolling around with Tiffany. Well, I can get me a young play toy too. Two can play this game. John, you want a drink? You want a beer?" They fussed and went back and forth for a few minutes seeming like they were trying to rekindle the flames. She grabs him a plate of food as he sits down. I'm so confused at this point, but then it clicked.

Ok I'm going to make this short and sweet. The jewel I learned from this was so crucial, I'm glad I learned this in my earlier years because I paid attention to this from that point on. First, I got up and told her I'll be back, I had to make a run. I didn't get the panties, and the next day at work, this woman wouldn't even look at me. To this day, she hasn't spoke to me but, her and Hercules are still together. She used me. She found a well-mannered, younger man that appeared to be on his A game and having things his way. She found someone that she could make her "ex" jealous with. She didn't like me at all. She used me to get to him and when I realized this, I realized that some women will throw you into a situation not thinking about the potential dangers it could cause. Her thinking with her emotions put her in a "I don't care about anything" state of mind. She was willing to take me, an innocent young man and throw me into a potential treacherous situation all to prove to her ex that she can get someone young as well. She wasn't thinking that I could have been scared out of my mind and shot this big intimidating guy. If this would've happened a couple of years later, it's possible that could have happened. She didn't think about maybe Joe would be so mad, he might come in and attack me. She didn't care. Obviously, he has been physical with her before by the way he grabbed her. Her response to him grabbing her was not out of surprise either, like she knew he was about to knock her head off. So, my takeaway from this experience was that people will throw you under the bus for their benefit. They won't care about how they lead you on and what feelings you will develop from their actions. Especially a married couple. You never want to be in a love triangle because in the end, you will lose.

You need to look out for yourself because no matter how someone may appear to care about you, they may have a whole different agenda that can hurt you. When people have their feelings involved, there is no telling what someone might do. People will use you for various reasons. Some people can't see past their own feelings. They let their emotions cloud their judgement. Now this whole situation could have ended up sticky. The issue with the two love birds was this: Bobbie caught him cheating with a younger woman. She wanted to get back at him, so she decided to come on to me. It worked because I was wet behind the ears and fell for it. She knew he was going to call while I was there. What a joke this whole ordeal was. I saw this couple about a week after this whole little incident. They were together dressed up on a Sunday morning. I assumed they were on their way to worship the Lord. I guess I helped them get back together, without even knowing. Lesson learned.

Jewel 2:

Watch Your People Who Use Mood-Altering Chemicals

I was introduced to crack cocaine when I was 5 years old. No, I didn't use it. My stepfather was a drug addict. Before I understood exactly what drugs were, I learned how to navigate around drug users. Have you ever had that feeling where you had to walk on eggshells around certain individuals because you didn't know what version of them you were going to get? Well, I had to at an early age. At 5 and 6, I had to survey my surroundings before I walked freely around the house. I had to observe individuals that were around me before I made moves. Sometimes, it was like I had to "check the temperature" of individuals. My stepdad was very abusive. When you are in situations where you are around an individual that sporadically flips moods with dangerous behaviors, you learn quickly how to move. I guess you are born with survival instincts that help you maintain awareness, and you navigate accordingly. During these early years of life, I was exposed to several drug addicts. Some would come over, or I would travel with my stepdad to gatherings where they would congregate and use their drugs. It would baffle me watching these adults flip moods in the matter of seconds. It was like you never knew what was going to happen.

With my stepdad, you would get several personalities. You would get the guy that would be a tyrant around the house ranting and raving about a piece of lent on the floor, or you would get a very calm and gentle guy that would smile and be quite easy to talk to. I liked those easy-going conversations. They made me feel like I had someone in my corner that I could turn to. Well, I couldn't get too comfortable with those feelings because I would have to be in defense or attack mode the next minute, depending on what drug he was using for the day.

My early years were consumed with feeling like a young psychologist, and I would "diagnose" every adult I came across with a disorder. I would study their moves and listen to the words that they would say. I would pay attention to their appearance. I would look at their mouths actively looking for a twitch or any movements that would indicate to me that they were using. I got particularly good at understanding what drug was being used. Obviously, looking at their red eyes would either indicate they were high on weed, or maybe tired from a 3-day binge of smoking crack. If they were nodding off, it was a good possibility heroin was their drug of choice. If they were short and irritable, they might have been going through withdraw. I got so good that I could usually tell when an adult was about to fire up a cigarette, because I could sense their urges. Sidenote: what I have mentioned so far is the advantage I received from sitting around adults being involved in grown conversations. I know a lot of us raise our children with the thoughts of not having our kids around grown folk convos, and I understand. There are plenty of reasons why it's not a good idea for young kids to be sitting around listening to adult convos, especially around the wrong adults. But there are also advantages. One advantage is that our kids are sponges. They pay attention to adults very well. As a child, for me it was beneficial because I learned ways of understanding. Understanding is important. I understood drugs make people act differently from their normal selves. You need to know and understand a little of the good and a little of the bad. Or maybe I should say a lot of the good and a lot of the bad. You are in a situation where you must be humble because these adults know more than you. To each is own, and you must make the right decisions for your child since you are the parent, however, look at it from the perspective of your child being educated by the world around them. It might be a good look. Anyway, back to topic.

Developing these observational skills early in life helped me along my 40 years of interacting with people. I'm never knocking anyone that uses mood altering drugs regardless of the drug of choice. I understand in this world people cope and get by the way they learn, and these drugs are very addictive. I've seen people in very so-called high places get taken under by the powers of addiction. This chapter is not to down addicts, but more to understand your surroundings and understand there are characteristics that are usually consistent with people that indulge.

So many people are living through this world with real life issues, whether they're from trauma, chemical imbalances, or effects from early drug usage. Some ease the pain by medicating through these habits of addiction. We are all around drug addicts because they are everywhere. Some of our friends are using drugs and we may not even know it. Some of our close co-workers or neighbors may be on a downward spiral from drug addiction and we don't know it until we see them hit rock bottom. Addiction is real and it can grab ahold of you so fast, you don't realize it has taken over until it is too late.

I've been around some weed smokers, and I can instantly tell they smoke because their short-term memory is gone. Or they lack the consistency of thoughts they had from conversations before. They become very irritable when they don't have their weed. I've seen a direct correlation with alcohol and depression. I had a friend that would be so enthused and motivated Monday through Thursday, and they would talk about all kinds of ideas they want to do and explore, but that weekend comes around and they hit the bars and next thing you know they are telling you how they slept all of Sunday because of a hangover. Ideas they once had go right out the window. So judging is not the answer. Understanding people and how they move is the motive. Understanding your surroundings and how to not be surprised when you run into an acquaintance that is exercising a typical characteristic of a drug abuser.

Know how to distance yourself from people when their addiction becomes dangerous. Know how to encourage people to keep their head up and be the friend that can be comfortable without drugs around. Use your senses to detect behaviors that are unhealthy. Knowing how to move around and not get caught up with certain individuals may save your life. Times often call for people to have their space, so give distance when needed. Make sure when you call yourself a friend, you are here to talk and try to uplift as much as you can. With anything and everyone, you must set boundaries though. One thing that is typical with drug abusers once the addiction takes over, is they become manipulative and very deceitful. They tend to care about the drug and the feelings they crave more than anything else. They will use you and misguide you. Unfortunately, there is only so much you can do because until they make up their mind they are done, they will not stop using. It doesn't matter if they go to several treatments, counseling sessions, lectures, etc. Until an addict says enough is enough, they will continue to use and destroy anything in their path including themselves.

Jewel 3:

Embrace You. Your Differences Will Open Doors for You

It's easy for me to say I'm different. For as long as I can remember, I've been made fun of for my characteristics. My red hair gets me called "ginger". My freckles used to get me called "strawberry". My light skin used to get me called, "white boy." My nappy hair used to get me strange looks. My "black voice" used to get me confused looks, especially from people that just met me. I've always had a little something different going on. For years, I struggled with this. I would think, "why me? Why do I have to stick out like a sore thumb? Why do I have to be so different?" When I was growing up in Des Moines, Iowa, biracial kids were rare. Nowadays, everyone is raising biracial kids. We are quite normal now and that makes me smile. This issue as a young boy through middle school and high school shaped a lot of my thoughts. I found myself early in school, not wanting to fit in. I didn't grow up with a tv, so I couldn't relate to shows everyone would talk about. Most of my time as a kid was spent writing, or outdoors playing basketball. When I would hang with my friends, I always had the lightest skin, unless there was a rare occasion of a white boy being around. After years of being groomed and conditioned to understand I was different, I started to get more comfortable with my appearance. I would often chuckle when I met someone because of their confused look on their faces. It started to be a fun game to me. I sometimes had to laugh to keep from crying because I didn't fully accept who I was. When you don't fully accept yourself, you create barriers. You work against your own being. We oftentimes make our situations harder because of how we feel about ourselves. The worst part about this is, we allow others to shape and mold our opinions of ourselves, but why when their view of us is very tainted and limited? They only get a glimpse of who we really are.

These people that judge us have insecurities of their own. Mostly everyone has some insecurity about their self. Our insecurities will not hinder us from the riches of the world, but the way we feel about them will. Out of the billions of people on planet earth, maybe four people care about your insecurities. That is how insignificant your "defects" are to the world. Embrace your differences so you can get out of your own way and take your life to the next level.

I switched up my thoughts and grew from them. I understood that not many people look like me and this is a good thing. You can use your "mishaps" to your advantage. Confidence is the biggest key to success. When someone realizes how confident you are in your skin, it will put you at an advantage. The confidence that you show overpowers any insecurity that you have. The confidence that you show will open doors to opportunities that will end up falling in your lap. The confidence shows from the inside out. How are you going to hate a part of yourself when you were created unlike anyone else in the world? That difference that you see, or feel is your uniqueness. Your unique characteristics are the tools to help you empower yourself and your surroundings. There is a reason why you have that “imperfection.” You were made strong enough to go through life with it and it is a part of your calling. Whether you feel too short or too tall, either way, you were created equipped to handle it. However, you are built is not a crutch enabling you to not give life your all. Live a less stressful life embracing you.

Jewel 4:
Energy

I believe this jewel is worth more than gold, so it was very intentional to put these words into this book. The understanding of energy is valuable. Nothing in this world outweighs energy. Nothing breaks energy. Energy is never destroyed, only transferred. This fact makes energy extremely powerful. You can literally add great value to someone's world with the energy you possess. You can help change someone's life with your energy. It is up to you whether the change is positive or negative. It is up to you because you control your energy. You are responsible for the "bag" of energy you have. Your energy can be the most beautiful thing in the world, brightening up rooms and hearts, just like the sun. Or your energy can weigh you down and drain the life out of your surroundings. Think about your life and reflect for a second. Think about someone you've met over the years that instantly made you brighten up and smile. This person might have walked into the room full of people, and most of you felt the weight of the world lift. The room got brighter, and everything seemed ok for those moments. That's energy! Or think about the time when you were around someone in their lower moments and suddenly you felt exhausted after talking to them. They drained you. The low vibrational energy transferred to you, and it made you want to take a nap. This is real. You can see energy. You cannot see it through the air, but you can see the vibrance on the carrier, which is you.

Before I learned about my personal energy, I walked through life with a powerless strut. I was unaware, blind, and ignorant to the fact that how I appeared to others reflected my energy. My energy was a direct correlation to my culture (one's way of life). I would move around the business world, meeting with investors, potential clients and colleagues and would be confused as to why I'm not striking more deals. My product was phenomenal, but my energy wasn't "moving the room." My energy wasn't sealing the deals. I wasn't selling the product AND myself. If you have a product, the potential customer must buy into you as well.

I started looking at the people around me. I started looking at how they react towards me. I started looking at how I felt about them, and my discoveries were life changing. I had a hustler's spirit, but I wasn't healthy. I was eating a lot of unhealthy foods. The only requirement was the food tasted good. I didn't care if it was unhealthy. I had ambition, and was deliberate, but my plan wasn't fully laid out. When your plan isn't fully laid out, at some point you lose direction, and it shows. Your confidence level isn't as high as it should be, so your energy lacks spark. Have you ever entered unfamiliar territory, or made the wrong turn somewhere? Your demeanor becomes tense. Your face instantly makes a confused look. Well, this is how you appear when you haven't created the entire map for where you are going. This map can change several times, and this is ok, but your focus just needs to be on the route of your map at that present moment. Everything in life needs tweaked from time to time, especially your routes.

There are three things that are crucial to the enhancement of your energy.

Firstly, you must be in love with yourself. Not infatuated, not obsessed …. IN LOVE! Have you ever been in love with someone? People can sense you are enjoying life. You have a special glow to yourself. Love yourself as well. Be a blessing to yourself. When you love yourself, you demand a certain reaction from people. You give people an example of how to treat you. Plus, you just feel great! How do you start to love yourself? For some, this will be a process. First, you must accept your past moments of shame or failure. You must understand that those not so perfect moments were a part of the formula to create the masterpiece you see in the mirror. If you didn't grow through what you went through, you wouldn't have the knowledge you have today. Accept you for you!

Secondly, treat your body right! Our bodies are led by our brains. Keep your brain healthy and vibrant. Exercise your brain by reading. Exercise physically at least three times a week. I would encourage more workouts, but three at the bare minimum. Get that blood circulating. Eat well. Most of your food consumption should come from the fresh produce section of your local supermarket unless you are growing your own foods. Fellas, I would encourage practicing semen retention for lengthy periods of time because this does our bodies so well. Get in tune with regular visits to the doctor's office.

Thirdly, positive vibes only. Yes, negativity is going to come in all shapes and sizes, but like I tell my daughter every morning, "keep your power." Learn how to deal with negativity the best way for you. Focus on your reaction to everything that is presented to you. If you keep yourself around great people, reading great books, listening to great music, watching great speakers, you will keep your energy great. At least when you notice yourself getting into a negative mood, you have points of references that are encouraging and uplifting.

Jewel 5:

Keep Your Momentum

A lot of what is written in this chapter is also in my book titled 8 Conversations to Have with Yourself. This is a very costly jewel, so I'm writing about it again. First thing first, let's break down momentum. Put simply, momentum is just movement. Constantly moving, whether physically or mentally. When you think of momentum in this term, it is easy to understand that you are in total control of your momentum. However, there are times when you give that control away, and you aren't even aware of it. How many times have you thought of an incredible idea, and we must ask someone's opinion? You don't even have the whole idea or concept completely thought out, but you feel you need to tell someone IMMEDIATELY because you are so excited. Your momentum is leading you in an intense way. So, you rush to the nearest phone to call your co-worker, business partner, spouse, brother, sister, or dog. With all the enthusiasm and energy in you, you pour your heart and ideas out all over this person, only to hear a dull and/or negative response. Now there is a difference between constructive and positive positions, and just downright negative and pessimistic positions. All you hear from this individual is negativity and it immediately kills your vibe. You start second guessing your own thought that was so overwhelmingly a "for sure win." This is when you must take a second and realize that you are CHOOSING to move slowly, or not move at all. Next thing you know your dream is silenced and overshadowed by this individual's "that won't work" attitude. It happens all the time for me and others. I can bet this has happened to you as well. This is called a shift in momentum. The euphoric feeling your own thoughts brought to you was bamboozled and shot down by someone that just simply didn't "catch the wave". They didn't see all the positives that you saw and THAT is perfectly ok.

It's not their dream, their vision, nor their idea. What is NOT ok is you giving your power away! What do I mean by this? It is simple. God gifts you with several ideas and visions and paints pictures that become clear as day. IF you put the right energy towards them. Once you transfer the energy to someone (by telling them your idea) that isn't very receptive, you must recognize that THIS is ok and take your energy back! Don't allow someone to "kill your vibe" or drown out your vision. Take it back and keep the momentum on high. Keep MOVING! I know, it is tough. Especially when you tell someone that you value about your great idea and they "shit" on it. But hey, you need to realize early that people don't see the same way. Just because there might be a mutual love between the two of you, doesn't mean they will automatically feel what you are explaining. It's human nature, get over it. That is why there are several hundreds of brands of the same products. Go to your local grocery store and walk down the potato chip isle, you will see several different brands of chips to appeal to several different audiences. There is something for everyone, and your ideas are no different. 7 billion people in the world and all you need are a couple hundred thousand lol. Keep your Power. Control your momentum. Tell yourself to keep moving forward. At times, you might not even move forward, just laterally, but this is ok, if you are moving. There are several other ways you can kill your momentum. The core of these reasons come from your own toxic and negative thoughts. If you are trying to motivate yourself, stay in a positive light because the moment you tell yourself anything that is negative, you take a chunk out of your momentum. You will start to move slower, think of distractions, listen more to others, Drown your own positive voice out. You might be having a bad moment and let it destroy your whole day and now you are wishing you had at least 12 of those hours back. It happens. Over and over. We are human. The key is to recognize these behaviors and nip them in the bud early so you can stay above the water and maintain a mindset of excellence. Even in a life crisis, your mindset will make or break you. You cannot have a bad day, only bad moments. Life crisis, such as death, relationship break ups, friendship feuds, automobile breaking down, fired from jobs, kids causing stress, etc. All are difficult to deal with. You might have had a great day in your car detail business. You cleaned 10 cars at 200 dollars a pop. At the end of the day, you are smiling on your way to your car to go home and your car won't start. You live on the other side of town and now you need to figure out how you are going to make it to work in the morning. Handle it! This is a part of life. You might have to take everything you just made and put it into your car, but don't lose your momentum. Don't use this car "crisis" to cancel the three appointments you have in the morning. Those three appointments help you keep your momentum (movement) high. Any slack up will cause you to lack sooner than later. Keeping your momentum high is tough work. It takes tremendous focus and discipline. Though you can do it, it will require you to do a few things. One, it will require you to evaluate your circle of friends and family. You must evaluate the people around you and put them in categories. Nothing is wrong with doing this. You love all your people, but you can't "invite everyone to the party." You can't tell your cousin John about a great business idea you have and expect great insight from him if he has never experienced business. Well, you can tell him, but understand who you are talking to when you get a full response, understand this is ok and KEEP MOVING! Respect other people's opinion, but don't let their thoughts consume you into drawbacks.

I was listening to multi-million-dollar real estate investor Grant Cardone on a podcast recently. Now he makes millions of dollars, guys. Something that he said caught my attention. He said sometimes at his seminars and events, he would go to the back of the room and set up tables and sell $2 items. Now why would a "super rich" guy spend his time selling $2 items, when he is getting several thousands for every event. He said that it adds to the circulation. What I gathered from it is valuable. I often have this same mindset, and this mindset is to keep your momentum flowing. It's not about the little two dollars that you are making. It's about the constant flow of your energy working for you! Hey, I sell books and to me, I've been successful.

But I will also pop my trunk and sell items that I have purchased at a wholesale price, so I can keep my natural energy flowing. I don't stop moving. You must move in this world and find what works for you. Some people are comfortable with their salary or however much money they make, and they feel they are ok. This lifestyle feeds their momentum. Some might look at these moves as you are greedy, or money hungry. Others might look at it as you are trying too hard. Others might look at it like…wait, let me stop! Who cares what other's think? Let them think whatever they want. Most people think with their insecurities anyway. Let them have that. You have an empire to build, and it is your responsibility to do so. No one else is responsible for you. No one else is paying your bills. Take your time and MOVE with it!

Jewel 6:

Be Alone

You were NOT born into this world by yourself. You had your mother obviously laying there, and I'm quite sure you had a few doctors playing a vital role in the success of your birth. You were born with a support system. This support system might have been small and short lived, but it is what it is. Now, oftentimes shortly after your birth, you may have been put into an incubator, or a nursery to lay alone. While you are laying alone, your loved ones come to the nursery window and take pictures and smile at you. Your mother may request the nurses to bring you to her from time to time if she is feeling up to it. Your mother may also protect you from people and their energy and germs, and not allow certain people to hold you. Well, here is my point. There are times where you need to be alone! It is rejuvenating. These times charge your battery. Yes, loved ones are important, and you should spend time with people. Interaction is important. However, a lot of us don't know how to be alone. A lot of us won't even go out and enjoy an evening in OUR OWN city unless we have someone with us. Standing alone is powerful. Being alone can create a fresh world for you because you become in tune with yourself. You are learning you and learning the world around you at your own pace. You have minimal distractions from others.

I have hundreds of acquaintances. I have some valuable friends in my life. Some I talk to every week, some I talk to only a few times a year, but these are solid relationships. I love when we get together and converse about anything and everything. However, you aren't going to talk to me every day. I don't care how good of friends we are; I don't care if we are lovers, we probably aren't going to talk every day. I love my "me time". I love being by myself. Listen, I have traveled all over this United States hundreds of times by myself. Some might think I'm crazy for some of the dangerous areas I have put myself in alone. I take the kids on vacations every chance their schedules allow, but a lot of times I travel for business. But I see exactly what I want to see, I visit the places I want to go, and I think a lot about what I need to think about. I don't have someone persuading me to go here or there. I don't have the thoughts of someone else distracting my flow. Don't get me wrong, I love group travels, and the intimate travels with a lady friend, but SOMETIMES you need that one-on-one time with yourself.

For years, I was a party guy. Of course, I was because I was a night life promoter for years. Some of my buddies would call me to see what I'm doing that evening and we would all go out. I would ALWAYS meet them there. I would never have passengers with me. That's not how I roll. I like walking into places by myself and I like leaving by myself. There is a great benefit in being on your time. Nothing against the guys. I love all my people to the fullest, but I like being on my own.

For a more serious look at this topic, let's focus on the jewel. Yes, you were not born into this world on your own. However, human beings are grafted and equipped with the tools needed to survive and SUCCEED on our own. We were gifted with a brain full of discernment. We have the ability to think and learn. We have physical features and elements that will get us beyond a bear in the forest. We all battle internally, and we cope with our issues oftentimes on our own. Sometimes we need assistance from others, and nothing is wrong with that if you need help from time to time. However, a lot of you develop a dependent nature in others, and that's where your issues come in. Every time something comes up, you look outward for help, advice, strength, love etc. God gifted you with these attributes. You can give yourself advice because you are given the ability to learn and research. You can give yourself love and strength because you have these characteristics in you. Some of us are in relationships because we don't want to be alone. You'd rather go through physical or verbal abuse because you feel it's better than being alone. You should change your perception of being alone. It's not so bad. Now, I encourage being in relationships that are healthy. Being in a relationship that adds value to you is a tremendous blessing in life. But don't get stuck thinking that is the end all be all. Don't think down on yourself if you aren't head over heels in love with someone, or if you don't have a partner. I believe in order to be in a healthy relationship with someone, a certain amount of alone time first is necessary. We must figure ourselves out to a great degree before we tackle a relationship with someone else. Self-development requires time with self and only self. Self-development is necessary for growth and growth is required when dealing with all things. Often, we move backwards and try to figure out someone else before we know ourselves. We as adults already have a disadvantage with our time because a huge percentage of our time is working on creating a decent living, so we barely make time to learn ourselves. I hear people say all the time, "nobody is helping me", "I got to do this all by myself"' like it's a bad thing. Well, people aren't obligated to help you, and oftentimes help comes with strings that can put you at a disadvantage. How great do you feel when you have accomplished a task solely on your own? Doesn't it feel great? Live that sometimes. Value that more and more. Be alone and empower yourself.

Jewel 7:

Several Different Minds in This World! Prepare Yourself For Many!

Years ago, I was talking with a friend about going to school to obtain a business degree. He asked me why I would go to school for a business degree. I told him because I want to be a businessman, obviously. He told me not to go to school for business. He looked at me after he chugged a gulp of coffee. "If you want to be a businessman, instead of going to school for business, you need to go to school for psychology. You need to know how to deal with different personalities. You will also be able to diagnose issues in people that you need or are around you. You need to understand body language, etc. You learn business by being in the field and doing business, not in a classroom."

This made so much sense to me. I didn't understand it then, but I utterly understand it now. 11 years into legit business and it has been ups and downs. Not because of my business products or numbers, but because of the inconsistencies of people. Not because of my business savvy, but because of the lack of acknowledgement of emotional IQ in people. There are so many reasons people get offended. You can walk into a situation thinking you are doing a great job, and someone is hurting from the actions you took, and you had no idea. Some people need to be recognized. Some people need encouragement. People need affirmation. People need counseling. People need love. Now, the extent people need these things vary, and this is where it gets tricky. Know your audience. Know your surroundings. Know who is who. If you are going to have people eating at your table, really get to know them. Get to know what ticks their tock. Unfortunately, I've had to learn the hard way. When I first started my business, I figured I would have to switch up from a street mentality to a more sophisticated one. I treated people with respect, and that didn't go a long way. I still treat people with respect of course, but it's a different approach. I need to get to know the individual now. I study their ways before I lock a deal. Before, I thought everyone in business thought alike. I also thought there was a specific way to do business that everyone involved knew about. Boy, was I wrong! There is a universal law in some areas, but it's obvious more than a few are not practicing these laws. Your emotional IQ must be high. You must be able to spot out people that cannot separate their emotions from numbers. Business is business and it must be ran as such. You must put together some tests for people that you will be working around. You must put everyone through tests. Depending on the results of the tests, you then treat them accordingly. Once you diagnose the results, don't change your stance on how you treat them unless they show you a tremendous amount of change. You also need to understand how you react and move. Some people are motivated by money. Believe it or not, most people aren't motivated by money. When you think about it, this makes sense. Human beings were brought into this world with feelings and passions. You were born with the ability to love, hate, be jealous, envious, etc. You weren't born with the know-how to manage money, or run a business, or any other man-made creation. You had to learn how to do these things. This is why you see some that go hard for dollars, and some that do not. Respect people and accept everyone for who they are, and where they are. Learn how to work with people and try to avoid intolerable behaviors that create bad situations.

Jewel 8:

Give Respect, You Get Respect

Somewhere there is always an individual tougher than you are. You must understand there are also a lot of cocky, hot headed individuals running around out here that would love to grab you and wrap you up into their misery. I often say anyone that is willing to jump off the handle and jeopardize their well-being and lifestyle for a stranger, is lost and maybe miserable. They may lack purpose. No one who enjoys life and respects others is going around being judgmental, disrespectful, or rude. It is true that most of the time, you get back what you put into the universe. It doesn't come back exactly how you dish it, but it comes back. If you walk around with a chip on your shoulder, someone is going to invite themselves to try and knock it off. It's just the way it is.

If you must be respected in order to show respect first, this says a lot about you. You must understand you are constantly showing others how to treat you. Respect usually goes a long way. The energy you put out is the energy you receive back. It is your responsibility to show who you are by showing what you are about. If you must get respect in order to reciprocate, this shows you don't respect yourself to a high enough standard. Respect is earned…by you! It's 360 degrees of completion, meaning everything around you is to be respected, until someone shows otherwise. "Respect is earned, not given." The person who coined this phrase must have been one low vibrational soul. This man/woman must have been in a dark hour of life, lashing out because he/she was wronged. Sorry for whatever happened to you, but this is not the way. Imagine going through life spending precious time trying to determine who to respect and who not to respect. That must be a stressful lifestyle. Since when do we live our lives according to how someone treats us? That "matching energy" is a follower's lifestyle. That lifestyle means that anyone can come along and persuade you to lose your cool, your composure, your power because of someone else's low energy. Once they cross your path with that low vibrational energy, you are willing to reciprocate it. I get it, I understand. I'm not saying take any disrespect. By no means am I saying lay down. However, I am saying control your moments. Control who you give your power to. Control your energy and keep it on high. The way you carry yourself and treat others speaks volumes.

How many times have you heard treat people the way you want to be treated? 90% of the time, when you show respect, you get it in return. You are teaching the people you encounter how to treat you. There is an aura that is over you that says great things about you. Your demeanor demands respect when your demeanor shows respect. Respect is given, yet make sure you take it away if it's not deserved. I learned along my journey; a smile gets me more than a mean face. When I walked around with my shoulders down, more relaxed and with a smile, it seemed to be contagious, so I continued to do this. It took me awhile because again, I grew up in the '90's. This time period was all about looking hard and walking around like you would kill a bear with one bite. I experienced most of my confrontations during this time period because of the demeanor I instilled in myself. A lot of people walking around in this world are ready to match your energy. They are ready for confrontation and are "wishing you would" take it to a level of disrespect, so they can put their bad vibes into the air. Give respect and make them earn your disrespect. You will live a healthier and more rewarding life If you move how you want to move.

Jewel 9:

More Rewards in Winning Than Being a Superstar

I have been on both sides of the coin on this one. I've been the superstar and I have played the backfield. Honestly, I can say there are pros and cons to both, however the preference boils down to what are you looking for in life. You need to make some decisions on what is more important to you. Is it important for you to have validation from your peers? Do you need acceptance? Do you just want to see a win? Are you a team player? These are valuable questions that need answered before you take a step to either be the superstar or the winner.

When I first started my marketing company, TeamStrong Inc., I wanted to build a huge team. I had several round table meetings with several people and shared my vision and dreams with many. I realized quickly that some people were more enthused than others, and some people had agendas that did not align with the benefit of my business, or me personally. I learned that everyone cannot go on this long journey of learning through trial and error how to be successful. See, I was young and did not know that the understanding of people was more important than any number on a piece of paper. It is imperative to learn the moves of the people that you choose to have around you. Anyway, that is another subject. Let's get back to the topic at hand, and that is YOU. But first, let me explain my logic. I'm working hard learning the ins and outs of business, but I quickly find out that since this is my baby, I must run it like it is. I must cradle my business and protect it. But most importantly, I must sell my products. I must be out in the forefront and let my presence be known. I must walk in these rooms and rub shoulders with fellow winners to make a play and keep winning. It was tough because some might look at this as a pro, but I looked at it as being work. I am extremely social at times. I love being around people in those seldom moments when I want to be around people. Most of the time, I like to be by myself, or with a couple of others. I was not always comfortable talking aloud, as many of you know that have read prior publishings of mine. I would cringe when it was time for me to take the lead and show my teeth. I hated being the center of attention, but most times, since this was my company, I had to be a superstar. I had the responsibility of playing each role of the organization. At times, I was the only instrument in the company. I would have to promote an event, print tickets, sell tickets, manage the comedians, book the comedians, type out the contracts, pick up the comedians from the airport, reserve their hotels, raise the money to book venues, etc. All of this had to be done, but at times I was a one man show. So of course, during the shows, some of the comedians on stage would give thanks to "John Martin" for bringing them to Des Moines. Of course, on social media, folks would say thank you to "John Martin" for bringing entertainment to Des Moines. They very rarely said thank you to my team. They very rarely said thank you to anyone besides me because I was the one that they saw running around all over promoting, putting up posters all over town and selling tickets. This is a lovely thing IF that is what you want. If you want the "shine" that this brings, more power to you. For me, I'll pass. I don't want that added "shine". Knowing what I know now, I have benefitted more from playing backfield positions in projects that I have helped create. There are people out there that hate seeing you "win". They hate the love you receive from others. They start to know too many of your moves, and you become an easy target for whatever they want to do to you. When things go bad, it's all your fault. When things go well, you have 70% of the people loving what you do. That 30% is a huge percentage for negativity. 30% negativity can be devastating to your brand and life. Everywhere you go, you will be looked at and scrutinized. The people closest to you in your life become a part of a lifestyle they didn't ask for and can be extremely uncomfortable for them. These are things you must pay attention to and consider when you are in the spotlight and making moves. Yes, if you want to be praised all the time for things, go for it. If you want to be told how great you are from several people that may or may not mean it, go for it. Go for what you want in life, and there is nothing wrong with wanting validation from your peers. Just understand it has been a proven characteristic and trend that people will build you up just to tear you down. On the other hand, I've had some of the best experiences of my life being the "unknown" guy in charge. I've set up several events in cities all over the United States, and I've had the privilege of sitting in the crowd, blending in and enjoying my time. No set up, tear down, or running backstage to check on lighting or anything. I was able to enjoy the show, whatever that may have been, whether it is a seminar, comedy show, nightclub event, etc. I got to enjoy myself. But I still won, and oftentimes, won big. Being able to be a vital instrument and factor in a creation of success is invigorating. This is what I crave. I crave seeing a product from start to finish. I had to learn what I wanted over time though. I had to play both fields. I didn't have the luxury of reading a book and having the author tell me to ask myself what I wanted and what was most important to me. I figured it out and nowadays I would rather help you through consulting, and help you develop the best of the best with YOU as the superstar. I'll sit in the crowd and enjoy the event, without the spotlight. I often find people that like the superstar appeal, and I wonder if they will ever grow out of that. If not, that is perfectly okay. People are driven by different things and when you are building a team, you must know what drives each individual person. You can bring out the best in someone if you just simply know what they are wanting, and you feed them just that. The most important takeaway from this chapter is this. You can have just as much power or more by being in the backfield. Model yourself after the structure of an octopus. An octopus has 8 legs, and they touch a lot of ground with those 8 legs. Use your tools and become able to make moves without a lot of chatter. Know when to take the spotlight and handle business, but also know when someone is more qualified than you, and hand them the torch. Play the backfield with the same mindset to win. My pops would always tell me there is a time to swim under water.

Jewel 10:

It's Not An Asset if It's Not Creating Wealth

I remember being in my late 20's, and thinking I was a boss. I put so much into my materialistic lifestyle because I wanted to look like something. I was so proud of myself for the material possessions I had. One year, I traded in a nice car I had put together with rims and paint job, to get a Dodge Magnum. Now this Dodge Magnum was a nice 2007 black beauty. I loved how it looked and I bought it with no rims on it. I couldn't wait to buy some 22-inch rims to put on it. I customized some expensive rims with a set of Vogue tires. I thought it was everything! You couldn't tell me anything. I would spend hours washing this car, because we all know how black cars need the upmost attention to keep them clean. I would drive down the street and at some intersections, I would get out and wipe the break dust off my tires so they would keep gleaming in the sunlight. I would pull up places and people would stop and stare at my ride and give me compliments. So much time and energy was put into my car. I would spend at least ten hours or better weekly just cleaning my car. Well, one day I got really drunk and blacked out. I woke up in the hospital with loved ones standing around me crying. I had no idea what happened. When I was told I totaled my car, I didn't believe them until I saw the pictures moments later. I couldn't believe it. Two things this moment taught me. Nothing is more valuable than life itself, and materialistic things come and go. The second jewel this taught me is what you see as value is not necessarily what the next man sees as value. You see, I put so much time and energy into this car. I put thousands of dollars into the rims and tires alone. Only for the insurance company to give me less than ¼ of what I paid for everything. I argued with my insurance agent telling him how valuable this car was to me, and he didn't budge. What I spent my hard-earned money and so much of my valuable time on was merely a piece of crap to my insurance company. From that day forward, I vowed to never think of a piece of metal as royalty.

One day in the past I was told never buy a house because I loved it. Never fall in love with a house. I think this was some of the best advice I've ever received. Not only has this saved me from making emotionally driven mistakes, but it has helped me gauge all my purchases and ask myself if the item is an asset or liability. Not only do I try and practice the rule, "if I can't buy three, I can't afford one", I also look at everything before I buy as "Is this going to make me money?" If no, I pretty much don't sweat it too hard. Here is what I mean. Let's say you are visiting a friend, and he tells you he is selling his shoe collection that you love so much. He gives you a sweet deal for ten pairs of shoes. The price he gives you is a good one. First, you must think if you can afford it. If he had three collections, could you buy all three? If not, I wouldn't even think about buying one. If you couldn't buy three, how soon could you take some money and turn it into the amount to buy three? Anyway, once you can buy three, go back to him and buy the one collection. Even my vehicles are low on the totem pole. I will rent them out so I can make money before I let them sit all day. Think about it. Your car sits about eight hours a day while you are at work. It sits another 10 hours at night while you are home or sleeping. If you are like a lot of us, you have a car payment. That car and insurance payment comes every month, and you get minimal service out of this vehicle. You bought it; did you say you love It? Did you fall in love with the color or the soft, comfortable interior? Well, now you love your car, and you are taking it to the car wash every week. Nothing is wrong with that. However, typically the resale value on cars is not close to what you bought it for. Most cars depreciate quickly. Now you are stuck with a big piece of metal that has turned into a headache. So, how about you rent it? Let's say your car payment is $400.00 a month. You put your car on an app program that has a platform for car rentals. Charge $200 a week. Now you get $800.00 a month. Now you have it rented, and you have another $400.00 profit. Profits can range, so you can make way more than just doubling. You can potentially make four times your car payment. Wouldn't you like to use that to pay your car off, or buy another car to rent? It is important to have a mindset of turning one into two, or even four. Once you get into a mindset like this, ways of doubling your cashflow will become second nature. We all need multiple streams of income, especially if we want to provide four our surroundings.

Jewel 11: Accountability is Power

Imagine going through life and blaming everyone else for your mistakes. Imagine everything happening to you is because someone else controlled the situation. Some of us walk through life like this. I remember when I first realized how toxic of a behavior this was.

I was 22 working at a call center. I sat next to this guy who was in his late 40's. He had a real big chip on his shoulder. One day, I was in the break room smoking a black and mild and here he comes with his coffee. He sits down at the table I was sitting at and starts to go on a 10-minute rant about how he has all these fines because of driving while barred. He said he is facing prison time because of this. I was in shock. I never knew someone could go to prison for driving while barred. He continued to talk and said, "yea and this last time I got stopped, the damn cop hit me with an OWI. He said I was drunk!" I then said, "well, were you?" He said, "maybe a little…but he had no business stopping me. He said he stopped me because I had a taillight out. Damn bastard! If it weren't for him, I would be able to take a couple hundred dollars and get my wife a b-day gift. I can't even do that now." Wow! This guy couldn't be for real. He decided to get in his car to drive while drunk, and his license was barred, but he didn't take any responsibility for this at all. He knew his wife's b-day was coming up, and yet he decided to drive a car while his taillight was out. Not a smart move at all, but let him tell it, it wasn't his fault. He is totally mad at the cop that pulled him over. This guy was in his late 40's and had the gray hair to prove it. But he wasn't smart at all. He has developed a mindset that so many of us have, and that is not looking in the mirror and realizing we have control over our lives. I, at 22 ended up telling this damn near 50-year-old man to man up and take responsibility for his actions. "Every move you made created your dilemma. You need to realize this, my brotha."

People that are always pointing the finger seem to be powerless over their lives. They subconsciously believe that everyone else controls them. Therefore, so many years go by before they act and build their lives. They feel they can't build because someone else will always mess it up. They take credit when they get a lucky "good" moment, but when something bad happens, it's everyone else's fault. There is no power in that. You cannot possibly live a desired life by putting your faults in everyone else's hands. You create your power by being accountable. Taking accountability is understanding YOU have the ability to build or destroy whatever you touch. Your decision making is totally your own. Once you realize accountability, you will hold yourself to a consistent responsibility and your life will change. You will start to sit in the driver's seat. Then you will get to adjust the seat and get comfortable. Then you will put the key in the ignition and take off, controlling your lanes. This is your life journey. Get my drift?

Jewel 12:

You Can Learn from a Baby

My son and daughter taught me so much about life in the first year of their lives. I mean, since my son was here first, he taught me about the natural process of growth. I saw him develop his motor skills. I saw him try to walk and fall repeatedly, but he would get right back up. He would get up and try to walk again with a refreshed approach, as if he didn't notice he fell 10 seconds before. Babies are extraordinarily strong and determined. My daughter taught me how to love her. She showed me exactly what she wanted and needed. When she needed a sippy cup, she gave a unique cry. When her diaper was poopy, she let out a frantic yell/cry. She would want me to hold her all the time. She taught me how to be more sensitive. She taught me about the beginning and evolution of a woman.

Do you know how I learned this stuff? I stayed open to learning. A lot of us adults close off our learning because we are at an age. I've met so many adults that look down at younger generations. They feel like the young can't teach them anything and this is where they lose out on opportunity. Don't ever think you can't learn from the next person. Matter of fact, train yourself to learn from every encounter.

Some of my biggest lessons I've held on to are from people that so-called had less than me. Also, I learned from people that didn't articulate as well as others, but I used my energy to meet them halfway, without judgment. I make a conscious effort to listen and get an understanding, regardless of how "awkward" a person looks or sounds.

A buddy and I were in Florida shooting some videos on South Beach. We were right in the middle of articulating some ideas and here comes a homeless guy walking up to us. I mean, this guy was so dirty, and his hair was so matted and thick with grease. He looked as if he hadn't showered for days. He didn't have any socks or shoes on, not a shirt. His chest was covered with caked on dirt, as well as spots of his face. He desperately needed a belt on, so he didn't have to hold his shorts up which were at least three sizes too big. I looked into his eyes and immediately saw pain. He started to mumble at us, and my buddy quickly turned his back to him. I told my friend to hold on and let's hear him out for a second. I always try to catch a story so I can learn from it, and this was no different. Unfortunately, this guy looked like he has been high nonstop for at least a year or two so I knew I would have to "meet him halfway" and really listen with intent to understand. My buddy reluctantly turned back around, and we both were facing this man that I could tell needed to get his story out to someone. I asked him what was wrong. A few minutes of listening to him spit out his story changed my life forever. I learned valuable lessons from him to this day I think about. He explained that he was a successful man in Connecticut. He has a wife and daughter, 401k, white picket fence sort of life and he was happy. He was stressed to keep up with his lifestyle of making tons of money and trying to keep up. He was working for a company that didn't value him, but he endured the pain day in and day out so he could keep a lifestyle his family wanted. Well one day his wife left him out of the blue and his daughter was taken by the state. He fought and fought for his 11-year-old daughter, and he failed. To make a long story short, he gave up and cashed out his 401k and caught a flight down to Florida and has been there ever since. Obviously, he has been killing himself daily with the drug usage, but he doesn't care. He doesn't even care if he has shoes on his feet. I asked him if he has talked to his daughter and he said he hasn't talked to anyone from back home in 2 years, since he moved down there. What a story. I took so much from him, and I learned that there is a breaking point for people. There is a level of stress that can take you to the limit and you can "tap out". How sad and disheartening that this man that had it all and worked hard to get it all let it all go. You can tell he loved deeply. He loved his wife; he loved his daughter, but he had to run for "cover" because the weight became too much. Anyway, I learned also that you gotta watch how attached you become to certain lifestyles. They come and go. Your mental health is the most important thing you have because it drives you. You must keep it together. So today, years later I think of this man often. I think of his struggles, and I use his story to keep me balanced. And to think I learned so much from a "bum". You never know who can teach you and give you a dose of life. Always keep your ears and eyes open for the truth. We can literally learn something from everyone. Don't ever be too big to not pay attention to the next man's story.

Jewel 13:

Make Sure You Are Ready Before You Start Getting Big Money

Do you know what is worse than not having any money? Having a lot of money and not being ready for it. Having money and not being ready for it can be damaging to your life. You must have the right mindset to have money.

I was young and money was coming easy because of some things I was involved in. Unfortunately, some of my extracurricular activities involved bad habits. Some of those bad habits were enhanced with the accumulation of money. Just think about a young alcoholic being able to drink as much as he wants, whenever he wants. How could alcohol be so plentiful for me? Because I had the money to spend on it. I started getting money to the point where I didn't have to worry about bills, so stress levels were down. That should be good, right? Not for some one that didn't have their head on straight. Money was dangerous for me. It allowed me to dwell in my immaturity. During this time period, it allowed me to enhance my bad habits. Instead of just drinking on the weekends, I started to drink every day, like every day was my birthday. Money allowed me to talk to more women, and unfortunately this was not good. Just because I had money that attracted women and gave me the opportunity to interact with more women, it gave me the green light to damage more women.

When you have money, you must have a goal for it. It is a tool for you to get what you aim for. You need a clear and precise route and intent. You also need to understand your bad habits and have a grip on them. If you have a gambling problem, the worst thing you can have is a great access to money. You will spend it. If you shop a lot, you may need retail therapy. Best believe you will have problems getting ahead if you don't control this habit. If you are a carefree party animal, and you live life like it's your birthday every day, that lifestyle will head you to a bad environment when you have more money. It opens access to the wrong people. When your mind is right, you have limits on who you surround yourself with. When you have goals in place and organized thoughts, your money works for you, not against you. You must know how to read people better when money is coming at an abundance. Man, people are going to come from all over to join you, with intent to use you.

They say money is the root of all evil. When your mindset isn't solid, it damn sure is. If your mindset has addictive ways that you haven't tamed, yes, it is. Let's say you have an addictive personality, and you use coke in a social setting twice a month when you go out to the clubs/bars. You start getting a nice flow of money and now you let your "guard down" a little and start enjoying life a little more. People are noticing you are getting more money because you aren't hiding this. You aren't controlling this. Your mindset isn't ready for it. Next thing you know, you are going from "kicking it" every couple of weeks to "kicking it" every other day. This leads to more indulgence. This leads to more cocaine.

Let's say you haven't learned how to say "no" to people. You are a pushover and being liked is extremely important to you. Well, you have an abundance of money, and now you are using this tool to buy friendships, or simply "help" people out when they are constantly asking for it. You are lending money out like crazy. Once the money dried up, you are back to the original feelings you had because those people aren't coming around anymore. Now you are back to square one. This happens.

Money comes and goes. You must develop and balance a mindset that understands this. Money is tricky when you aren't "ready" for it. It can drive you deeper into depression, drug abuse, debt, vulnerability, and even suicide. How many people have you known that killed themselves because they went from money to none? Plenty of people have got a taste of that fast access and couldn't handle it. This jewel is particularly important. Work on you before you slip into a slope of uncontrollable falls. Money will help you do anything your mind leads it to, so you must have brains to lead it. Your mental must be clear of a devil mentality. Understand that working on getting you to a place of knowledge, wisdom and understanding self will have money being your ally instead of your gateway to destruction from your demons.

Jewel 14:

The Accumulation of Fast Money Can Damage You

Let's continue talking about money for a second. There are several disciplined actions you need when it comes to money. The potential to create anything you want is plentiful. You can do anything you put your mind to. However, fast money can damage you, and your spirit.

When I found out I was going to be a father, I worked hard at a job putting in 40 hours a week. My son's mother was doing the same. We were living paycheck to paycheck for a while, but we had our own place and doing fine. It was surely stressful of course. We were young and just learning the ropes of being an adult. But the addiction of fast money haunted me. I would look at my checks as if they were trash. I would look at the amount of the check and then the hours I was putting in and it didn't make sense to me. I was used to making in a day what I was taking home in two weeks, and it was getting to me. You see, it's much more than the money, it's the mindset that you learn when you are getting fast money. Once you go the route of getting "money per transaction," instead of "money per hour", it is extremely hard to go back to "normal". I would ask myself why am I doing this when I could be making more in minutes. So, temptation got the best of me, and I started going back to my old ways. I didn't respect the 9 to 5 lifestyle. I grew frustrated with it and in turn started doing whatever I could to get that fast money rolling in. I was very productive and busy during this time period. I would work on getting my money accumulated by setting up plays and utilizing a team. Before you knew it, I was getting nice money. They say money attracts money. I believe this. The route of being dollar devoted lead to me being a manager of exotic dancers. Now during this time, I was hustling in the street and working a 9 to 5. I was working around the clock enjoying being productive. I felt like I was being accomplished. When people see you glowing and vibing in good spirits, they want to join you. So, it was easy for me to attract dancers, or strippers. For some reason, it was even easier for them to give me a large portion of their money. I had three girlfriends giving me approximately $1000 a week. I was making about $3000 a week just from their grind. Doesn't seem like a lot of money, but it is a huge amount when you aren't working for it. I was living the life. After about six months of the dancers being in my life, "taking care" of me, this is when the real issues started. I started to get careless in my personal life. My relationships were falling apart. I was partying heavier, which resulted in losing my 9 to 5 job. At the time I didn't care. I had a lot of money flowing in, so they could keep that 9 to 5. The biggest downfall was me getting lazy with my own hustle. Even though it was illegal, it is the mindset that the hustle brought along that kept me going. I no longer had that "go get it" spirit. I was lazy, getting up later and later every day. I got too relaxed in my grind and my team was dismantled. I even got lazy with the women that were paying me. I would oversleep when it was time to pick one up from the club. Or I would just leave town without saying anything. I was a mess. I totally lost my ambition to have things.

I have talked to several people that have come from similar backgrounds, and we all say the same thing. The hustler withdraw is tough. When you come from fast money, and you try to straighten up and work a 9 to 5, it is incredibly challenging. I ended up losing my sources of income and I had to work extremely hard to develop a go getter spirit again. I suffered depression from this, as do many others. This doesn't just happen from being paid from illegal activities. Anybody can fall victim to this. Most people that are driven can make it from the bottom with nothing. But when you get an abundance of fast and easy money, your ambition can be destroyed. Just watch yourself and put some money away. When you are getting fast money, make sure you have goals for your grind. Make sure you have a route to see your plans through. Determination is important. You need to remember the money doesn't last forever. After the money is gone, you still need that hungry lion. Might as well exercise and develop a habit of staying hungry. Don't ever get comfortable until you are ready to be comfortable!

Jewel 15:

Sex is a Drug

Do you remember your first sexual encounter? A lot of women I have interviewed did not enjoy their first time. A lot of men I have interviewed lead me to believe their first time was life changing. For me, I wanted more. Once I got my first real piece in high school (before high school, it was an awkward situation for me, so I'll explain in later publications), it was on! For a long time, that is all I could think about. In my early adulthood, the fellas and I would go out with the intent of scoring. Sometimes it didn't matter if I knew the woman or not, she had what I wanted, so I would pursue. This isn't any different than most people. We all go through a phase of intense sexuality. We are human. Some of us are being used and warn out by our own desires. If you have an addictive personality, you will fall victim to your sexual pleasures, and oftentimes end up in a predicament. Unwanted children, STDs, bad energy, toxic relationships, etc. Most of us have seen real examples from others, and still fall victim to sexual characteristics. A huge percentage of marriages fail nowadays because of sexual related issues. Sex can impact us in several ways, without us realizing it before it is too late.

First, realize what you have. You can't share it with everyone. Some can't handle it. Some will become too attached too soon. Some will become addicted to your potency. So, if you don't have yourself in check and disciplined, you won't even realize what is happening. You won't be looking for the crucial signs. Do you know some people use sex as their way of communication? Do you know some people use sex as their way of expressing "love"? It's true, most people have an agenda behind their actions. Sex is no different.

Secondly, when you have sex with someone, it's not just about you anymore. You are taking on baggage from your sex partner and you are also giving baggage. What is the baggage? Your aura.

It's your energy, good or bad. The transfer of energy is strong. You can be giving exactly what your sex partner needs. They may become obsessed. They may want you more than you want them, and they may be willing to go above and beyond to prove this. Watch who and when you involve yourself with this. It may seem innocent but look beyond your personal emotions and perceptions. Look at the bigger scope.

Jewel 16:

Play Dumb and Get Ahead

This rule has worked for me ever since I was a kid. There is more than one advantage to this rule, so pay attention.

Nobody expects anything from a fool. If you want to get out of extra duties and responsibilities, play dumb. Most will not want to invest the time to teach you more task, so you will not be granted those responsibilities. Oftentimes, your employer will tolerate you if you do the minimal requirements. For some people that is good. They don't want more responsibility. But let's get deeper.

Sometimes, you need to let people think you are not that quick of a thinker. This can be good in situations where you want people to show their true selves and true thoughts. When you become the dumb friend, you appear to be more innocent and less intimidating. People tell you things that they would normally package differently if they thought you were smarter. The guard comes down more often, and you get to scope the room at your leisure at a more discreet phase.

Not everyone is privy to the information that you know. Sometimes that information you know may not be in the best interest of the person you are in front of. Often, people in your life will try to play a position to get over on you. They have motives, and agendas. When you are a good person, your aura shows and to some you look like food. These people you may want to show a little bit of intelligence so you can stop them in their tracks. You don't want them to get too deep in their plans that they have an advantage.

Playing dumb and being dumb are two different things. Don't get so used to the role that you lose focus on when to turn it on and turn it off. You must be smart enough to recognize when to take advantage of this and when to "flex your muscle."

Also, it is valuable to oftentimes be the dumbest person in the room. This is when you can be the student and absorb the info around you to the fullest. Being the smartest in the room means you are in the wrong room because it's too hard to elevate to a higher level if you are constantly having to reach down and educate your surroundings. Be the dummy and let it work for you. Allow your eyes and ears to grab all the information you need.

Jewel 17:

Comfortability Can Kill You

The one time in my life when I was comfortable, it was more damaging than good. Unfortunately, I didn't realize I had a long life to live that required a lot more work to maintain the lifestyle I was enjoying. I was blinded by the moment of being relaxed. I was in a dream state of mind. I didn't realize the moment wouldn't last forever.

I remember when I had a rude awakening. This was a life changing moment for me, so let me explain. I was working at this call center, and I was sitting next to a guy named "Jim". Before we were sitting together, we were in the same training class. We would take lunch together and have great conversations. We kicked it off well. We grew to be great friends. He would invite me over and I hung out with him and his wife. He was excited to be settled down and working his job. I remember our first day out of training, he had a huge box of nick knacks he put out on his desk. He even brought a lamp to plug in and set on his desk. I mean, it took him like 45 minutes to unpack everything, from football cards, to autographed football jerseys. I couldn't believe how much he had on his desk. I remember thinking to myself, "why is he making this like his living room?" He had a picture of his wife and a recent ultrasound picture. His wife was expecting their first boy. Man was he happy about life. I loved seeing someone so happy and so enthused to work at a place I saw as a steppingstone for the moment. I knew I wouldn't be there long, maybe about six months tops. I wanted to keep moving and get something bigger and better. But Jim was married, content and ready for a career. I remember him often saying he would apply for a management position soon. I would ask him why he would want to babysit everyone. He would laugh and say, "man you are ten years younger than me. You will think differently when you get older." I received that well and looked forward to that day of happiness and wanting to babysit others. Anyway, make a long story short, two weeks before the due date of his son, Jim was fired for attendance. This was also before he was there for six months, so he wasn't eligible for unemployment. You should have seen the day the supervisor was packing his stuff up from his desk. The supervisor was just throwing his stuff carelessly in a box. I was looking in amazement on how some things can mean so much to someone, but so little to others. I felt bad for Jim because he loved what he did, and he was planning on staying awhile. Poor Jim. He was comfortable. He was the signature company guy. He even bought a hat with the company logo on it. He felt at home at his desk with all his loved possessions, for him only to be let go. How unfortunate to have a plan and believe in it so strongly that you are blinded. Blinded? Yes, getting comfortable in a situation that you don't control can damage you. Jim didn't have any control over staying at that job. So many of us put our all into some things that we do not have power over. From that day forward, whatever job I am at, I never brought any personal possessions. You would think it's an empty cubicle. It is not my place. I'm not getting settled in. Not only because I am disposable at any moment, but also because once you are comfortable, you stop realizing you are needed in your future. You still must continue to grind with blood, sweat and tears to set your future up. Once you settle down and relax, you become stagnate. You become complacent and then you become dependent. You no longer depend on yourself because you aren't the one rolling out the red carpet for yourself. It is someone else cradling you. Just like in Jewel "fast money can damage you" same outcome but different cause. Being uncomfortable has its rewards. Being uncomfortable keeps that fire burning, and motivation continues instead of death. Some may say not getting comfortable at your job may create a negative attitude. Well, I say if you have a negative attitude, that will shine through however you move. You still must keep your momentum high and your attitude moving towards happiness. Working on your goals outside and beyond your current position in life can help your attitude stay fresh and motivated. Your job isn't where you end, it's where you work and work towards your own goals of achievement.

It might sound crazy, but you must throw YOURSELF a curve ball sometimes. Life is a game and when you get tired, you start to lose. Look at any sport. When you are at your best game, you are fully energized. You have an irresistible hunger for victory. You want to win! You can't win when you are lazy. You can't win when you are distracted by nonsense. You lose your desire to win when you lose energy. You don't stay hungry because you are used to eating. These are examples of what comes from being comfortable. How productive are you after you eat a meal? How productive are you when you know you have a food coming every day and you aren't missing meals? What's the best way to see what you have? What's the best way to use what you are made of? The best way to see what you are made of is by putting your back up against the wall and fighting from the gut. When you are winning, it's easy to get comfortable. When you get to a level of comfort, most often you create a consistency of knowing you have a meal coming. This can be damaging at times because you lose the fire. You start skipping important steps that got you to where you are. Your effort slacks, and then you start enjoying your fruits of your hard work a little too much. Apart of enjoying your fruits is the comfort that you receive, so recognize the comfort, enjoy but don't overindulge. Look, I lived in a trap house as a shorty. I watched people destroy their lives for a piece of crack rock. I was in the middle of the struggle. And I wasn't comfortable at all. I hated it. A few of you understand and been there. So, what if I gotta knock myself down? I know how to rise. I know how to get hit. I've taken some good licks and so have you! Can't hurt no worse than what I've been through. So what if gotta take a loss? I ain't going to lose it all. I've proven I will get up over and over, and you will get up too. Our strength is within, and we have proven ourselves to be resilient.

Jewel 18:

Focus on Your moves, not THEIR Understanding

We all come from different walks of life. Our understanding of certain situations is shaped and molded by different experiences. These mind-altering "snapshots" can block understanding or catapult it. With this being said, of course not everyone has your beliefs or understandings. So, stop trying to convince the world about your visions. Once you put a vision into the world, the right people will gravitate towards your vision, and they will understand. It's not for everyone. I've spent countless hours over the years stressing trying to get people to understand my viewpoint. I would break down several different ways of communication, and for some these would work, and for some these wouldn't. We want everyone to understand us, don't we? The world wasn't built like that. Recognize the differences and keep moving forward. You will waste energy and time trying to convince someone, and at the end of the debate, you will lose. You will lose your piece of mind. You will lose heartbeats. You will lose energy.

There are over 8 billion people in this world. 8 billion different ways of thinking. Tolerate them and understand you have your own as well. I used to be an event planner and promoter. Comedy is one of my first loves. I started putting comedy shows together in Des Moines, IA. These were urban comedy shows that were mirrored after the Def Comedy Jam series in New York. They were showcasing the up-and-coming comedians all over the United States. The super funny comedians that just never made it big yet, and in my opinion funnier than the mainstream comedians that grew lazy in their craft. I would put the whole show together, contact and set up contracts with comedians, sell tickets and promote. It was exhausting at times. One thing I grew tired of was explaining my moves to people. Some people just didn't understand business, or they had different approaches. The different approaches were good to hear at times because I'm open minded. But most viewpoints came from people on the outside looking in and didn't have any clue. One big question I was always asked and sometimes ridiculed about was my decision to produce clean comedy shows. People liked the raunchy shows so much, they couldn't understand why I switched up. They didn't understand when I was producing these shows, I would rent out bars and event centers, so therefor I wasn't getting any of the bar sales. This comedy thing was fairly new to Des Moines. There were urban comedy shows before, but not as often and as a brand, so negotiating was at a disadvantage at times. However, when I started selling out urban comedy shows on a regular, here comes my biggest competitor. The biggest comedy club in the state started bringing urban comedy. They never did before, but as you can imagine they would win in that lane. At that time, I couldn't compete with them because they are a chain. They had thousands of emails to send mass emails that didn't cost them a thing. They get alcohol and food sales as well, so their profit margin was just too big for me to compete.

I had lot of momentum built up with this comedy thing, and it was growing. I saw the potential. But the bigger comedy club was bringing big name comedians, so they really threw a curve ball at me full speed. I thought quick. I took my show out of the bars and produced a family friendly clean comedy show at the Marriott ballroom. My thinking was to provide something for the whole family. I would have the same top-quality show with super funny comedians, but it would just be a show that was appropriate for the whole family without the raunchiness. I'm providing for the whole family, plus the bigger comedy club would never do this. They would lose their money maker, and that is the alcohol. Also, I was managing a young up and coming comedian that needed to perfect his craft and I believed learning to pace himself and pitch a clean set would build his arsenal and make him more poised and experienced. I survived the comedy war by staying volatile and versatile in a narrow market. But of course, some people didn't understand. At that time, I wanted to explain to everyone, and I got into arguments with some people. Some thought I sold out. Some thought I was trying to be a Christian. Some people just tried to find so much to say. But all I had to do was focus on selling my shows out. In a small city, you must stay on top of creativity and keep moving. You must stay on top of your game and in order to do this, you can't involve yourself in chitter chatter from folks that aren't at the table with you. Keep the voices that you listen to at a minimum. Hear all but limit the thoughts behind someone else's understanding. They are looking through a skewed lens.

Jewel 19: Pay Yourself First

This jewel is underestimated. It is simple and sounds so easy. But it really is overlooked by so many. I learned this jewel early but didn't always practice this and I look back sometimes with a frown because of it. So, let's look at the rule. They say when you get paid, take an amount and pay yourself before you pay any bill, or buy any of your wants. Sounds easy to do. Why was this so hard for me? When I first heard this, I was in my mid-twenties. I was working for a collection agency getting big bonus checks. You couldn't tell me anything, I was getting paid! I would spend my whole check though and didn't save anything. Then when I heard about this jewel, I tried it. I think I paid myself too much because I always ended up jumping into the stash. So, even if your check is 200.00 and your bills are most of that check, at least put a small percentage of it up. Maybe out of $200, you are only able to pay yourself $6. Do it and forget about it. Don't touch that money. $6 is not going to kill you. Figure out a way to leave the $6 alone and make up for it. This skill is so underrated because I don't think a lot of us see the other valuable lessons. For one, it creates discipline. If you are in a situation where you feel you need to dig into the stash because you are running low on funds, you can. But how empowering is it figuring out other creative ways to compensate for the money you saved. Another reason this is valuable because we are visual and if you see something growing, you can build a momentum from that. I don't care what anyone says, seeing your bank account grow is very satisfying and motivating. Before long, you will look forward to paying yourself first. Then, one day your "pay yourself" stash will be bigger than your checks. It is an achievement that will have you in a better position. If you lack the discipline to devote 10% to you, have it payroll deducted into an account you can't touch. That way you don't even see the small percentage. But after a while, you will be able to see what your compound consistency can create.

Jewel 20:

Understand How You Are Perceived By Others

Perception is valuable in life! Perception holds weight in everyone's brain, whether we want to admit it or not. The way someone looks at an object or an individual, tells how and what he would do to or about that object or individual. You better pay attention. The way someone looks at you will determine how they attempt to treat you. The way someone views you will tell you how they will handle you if times get hard. Or if you offend them, you might say you don't care how someone feels about you, but I'm here to say this. You might not CARE, but you better UNDERSTAND. If someone feels you are a threat to them, they will feed you with a long spoon. They won't let you close. They will feel intimidated in your presence. They might ask people questions about you to gain information to use against you one day. In their presence, they may even feel inferior towards you. These are examples of real-life interactions. The views a person has for you determines how far the relationship can go. Judgement sets in within seconds of meeting someone and from that point, you further determine what you think about this person. Whether you see an attractive man/woman and you are deciding if you want to give him/her your instagram info. Or you are a beautiful woman, and you get hit on multiple times a day from various people. You are approached by how someone based their opinion of you and how they view you. This is important to understand. It can keep you from being oblivious. Picture being a huge 6'4 350-pound giant that is on trial in a courtroom fighting for his freedom. It wouldn't be in his best interest to appear even more massive and intimidating by acting overly aggressive. But being self-aware, he might understand he needs to tone it down a little. Maybe wear light colors. Get a clean haircut. Look a little more presentable. He is already big and being big to some says violent. I'm sure you agree things like this are important to know, right?

If you want to be taken seriously, the event may call for a suit. If you want to seem more down to earth and personable, wear a sweater and jeans. I mean, you are rubbing shoulders with all your surroundings. You are passing people every day, interacting. You need to know how one feels about you, because in this day and age anything can be done. In this world, people can harm you from a distance. Rock your whole world from a whole different continent on earth. You might be out of there as easy as someone calling B4 on the game Battleship.

Let me use myself as an example to provide an out of body experience for you. You can visualize me. Maybe some of you can relate.

Do you know there are people in this world that think they know me, and they have a perception of me growing up with a silver spoon in my mouth. Like, I never struggled. Like I didn't live in a real-life trap house at 8 years old. Like I didn't have to stand in line for hours waiting on food commodities. Like I wasn't exposed to crack cocaine as a youngin. Like I didn't witness my mom getting beat on and couldn't do anything about it. Constantly in and out of the pawn shop trying to get a little for a little. All facts! Now, no matter if I'm in a business meeting talking to potential investors, or at a gas station in line and talking to someone that is planning to rob me, how someone feels about me determines everything. That potential investor might like my idea but may look at me like I don't deserve the investment. He might have looked at my social media and think my life is just so easy, and he may form an opinion of me based on this and say he doesn't want to invest. How someone perceives you determines if you get the job. It determines if that woman is going to invite you over to her house. It determines if they lie to you, it determines if they give you a good reference for a job.

Regardless, if you are a salesman and you have the best product in town. If that woman or man feels a type of way about you and it sparks a little emotion, he might shop with someone else that has the same thing to avoid you. You don't have to go above and beyond who you are. Don't fake anything. Be real and understand how people feel about your realness from their perception. Just understand, without emotion.

Because this is so important in life to understand, you must get in tune with your surroundings. It can cost you your life in certain situations if you don't learn your people. It can cost you a job. How do you get in tune? Get to know who you surround yourself with. One, you must be attentive. Pay attention to the jokes and the ha ha's. There is truth in every thought. Sometimes that bare truth is simply the fact someone said it. But that's truth. Anyway, pay attention to what's said about other people in your presence. It's important to pay attention to how other people treat your person in question. Is this person generally respected? Are people scared of them? These are all feelings people display in the most innocent and natural ways. Body language tells the story of how someone feels about you. Studies show when a woman is in front of you and she has her arms down revealing her open chest, she is comfortable around you. If she folds her arms, she may feel withdrawn. The easier you can make the people around you feel comfortable is a benefit. But on the reverse side of this, you need to know how to make someone uncomfortable. There will be certain people in your world that you will never want to be comfortable around you. Let's just say, since you paid attention to this certain individual, you understand he is jealous of you. You have seen the signs. You put a couple feelers in the water (feelers are people that are associated with you on the low. They blend in with the crowds and listen to people's reactions. People speak freely in front of these individuals ABOUT you because they don't know you have ties with them. They need to care enough about you to tell you what was said, and you make a mental note and move swiftly going forward.) Sometimes it is inevitable. You will be around someone that doesn't like you and wants to do harm to you in some way. You must keep these people uncomfortable. You can do this by staying unpredictable. They should never know your thought process or how you think. They can never learn your moves. Keep them guessing and eventually stressing because they can't figure you out.

Part Two of this book is up next. I hope you have received some value out of Part One. In Part Two, I discuss more topics that relate to parenting, business, bad decisions, guns and violence. I also discuss the power of social media and a lot of other things that I think I've learned over the years. So let's take a break, I'll talk to you all in a minute. ⍰

www.ingramcontent.com/pod-product-compliance
Ingram Content Group UK Ltd.
Pitfield, Milton Keynes, MK11 3LW, UK
UKHW020414250726
13967UKWH00007B/2639

9 781329 491885